WELCOME
TO HELL

Also by Tom Piccirilli:

WELCOME
TO HELL

A Working Guide
for the Beginning Writer

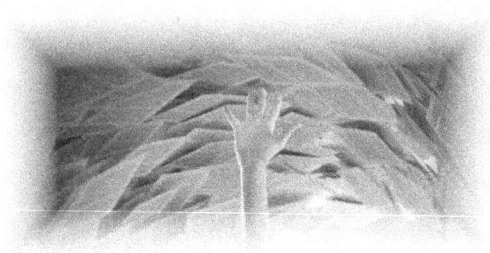

TOM
PICCIRILLI

FAIRWOOD PRESS
Bonney Lake, WA

WELCOME TO HELL
A Fairwood Press Book
Copyright © 2000 by Tom Piccirilli

Fairwood Press
21528 104th Street Ct E
Bonney Lake WA 98391

**See all our titles at:
www.fairwoodpress.com**

ISBN: 978-1-933846-83-5

Fairwood Press Second Edition:
August 2019
Also available in ebook

Cover image © Getty Images
Cover and book design
by Patrick Swenson

Printed in the United States of America

This one is for Michelle Scalise, Brian Keene, Mike Oliveri, Geoff Cooper, and Trey Barker. Extra special thanks go to Michelle for reading through this book in its earliest stages, and to Brian, who unwittingly gave me the perfect title. I'm also indebted to Patrick & Honna Swenson for making such tremendous efforts to bring this volume to life.

CONTENTS

INTRODUCTION #1

THIS IS NOT A HOW-TO BOOK. I'M NOT sure if I believe that writing can be taught, and if it can, I'm probably not the one to do it. Writing can, however, certainly be learned. I find most How-to books about the publishing field to be more annoying than ultimately helpful. Many of them state rules on what to do, what not to do, and how to succeed in three, fourteen, or thirty-one easy steps.

Outside of simple manuscript mechanics there are no fast or easy rules on how to produce solid stories and novels, how to sell them, and how to garner a professional career in writing. What works for one person won't necessarily work for another.

This is a guide to getting started, a

map of what pitfalls to look out for, and an outline of what struggles and achievements you can reasonably expect through the course of learning your art. If you get anything out of this small book I hope it's the idea that you should experiment with style, voice, concepts, and *musing* until you find what allows you to express yourself the best. Even after you find your narrative voice and hook and niche, you should still explore other venues and techniques to avoid stagnancy.

I'm going to talk about "the page" a great deal. Yes, I know we all work on computers now, and it would be more accurate for me to discuss "the screen" instead, but hey, poetic license and all that.

So, this book is written with a plethora of disclaimers. No, I'm not a millionaire or a bestseller or someone critically hailed to the four corners of the planet. I haven't sold to the movies yet, (not even to *Showtime* or *HBO*, damn it). I'm just someone who's been writing for about a decade now and been fairly successful at it, and I've made just about every mistake you can make in this field and hopefully learned from them.

That said, these lessons are meant as only a general guide to discovering what works for you in a difficult art and an even more taxing industry. This is an overview of what I've found to be elementary truths about the craft and business of writing. Truths that are often lost in the lavish dreams, mythology, and misconceptions of what it is to be a writer.

INTRODUCTION #2
*SO Who is This Guy With the Goofy Name
AND Why the Hell Should We Listen To Him?*

or

Pic's Tale of the Trenches

A LITTLE ABOUT ME.

I lucked into the business ass-backwards, and I paid the consequences for that luck. The first serious piece of fiction I ever wrote was my first novel *Dark Father*. I finished the opening fifty pages the summer I graduated college, sent an unsolicited partial off to Pocket Books—which breaks just about every rule of submission you can think of—and somehow the stars aligned correctly so that my manuscript wasn't immediately drop-kicked back into my lap. I got a call from an editor three days later, did a dance on the dining room table (I can do a hell of a *Tarantella* when inspired), and sold the book based on the sample chapters.

Sounds slick and simple, right?

Before I'd even fully completed the novel, my editor left the house and a new one came on board who didn't think much of it, my writing, me personally, or horror in general. When *Dark Father* came out it pretty much disappeared without a ripple.

They say the first book is the hardest to sell. After that you can cruise along the shoulder of life and just hand the finished novels in one after the other, watch them hit the shelves with startling regularity while you bask in the love and respect of the world, with hefty bank deposit slips scattered at your slippered feet.

Pardon me while I laugh myself into such a frenzy that I choke up my pancreas.

I watched my first novel get remaindered in a matter of months, and I spent the next several years writing novels I couldn't sell.

And you better believe that I also did a lot of lip-gnawing on sleepless nights, feeling like a failure and trying to rediscover the key that I'd lost without even knowing when in the hell I'd ever had it.

I eventually decided I needed to break into short fiction and follow the more traditional route of honing your narrative skills through your stories before entering into the novel arena. It took another year or so before I'd sharpened my craftsmanship to the point where I could consistently sell my work. This is what novelist Harry Crews calls "turning a corner." After selling thirty or forty tales, I'd turned the corner and returned to the books, edited and rewrote them, and managed to sell those off as well. The two halves of my career seemed to come together, and all because I went back to the beginning.

If you want to succeed you need to start at the most rudimentary aspect: the blank page.

And if anybody tells you that all you need is a lucky break, tell them to shove off.

Luck is about the worst thing that can happen to you in this biz, and it's no substitute for knowledge, experience, effort and skill.

FIGHTING THE GOOD FIGHT

or

*Surviving Rejection, Discouragement, and
the Fact that your Mother/Spouse/Children
Keep Screaming at you to Go Back
to College and Get a Real Job*

LET'S DEFINE AN IMPORTANT TERM here and decide what it is to write "professionally."

Professionalism is not merely an attitude. It's also more than a mind-set, and a hell of a good deal beyond a bad act put on by the tortured *literati* wannabes.

For our purposes, let's say that you write professionally when you've decided that writing is not merely a hobby, a performance or a passing interest, when it's not solely a dream or goal you've set yourself to attain in the far-flung future.

You write professionally when you regularly complete stories and submit them to the marketplace. The same holds true when you work on a novel with the hopes that when it's finished you'll send it out with the expectation of getting it published. *Soon.* Not in thirty-seven years when you retire and have nothing better to do but dictate your memoirs about your wild freshman experiences with your roommate Vegetable Fat Vinny, or when you finally decide to name names and blow the top off the Pez industry.

This is an objective you have a burning passion to achieve now.

Nobody ever said that to be a proficient, capable author you had to be well-paid or even successful, but you do have to be *working*.

If you rewrite one tale endlessly and never finish a second, then you've got no right to walk around claiming to be an author. If you jot stanzas of scribbled verse in your pocket notebook only so you can spout drunkenly to your girlfriend in the middle of a downtown club, then you ain't a real writer yet, kid, buck up and face the fact. If you have seventeen half-completed books in your trunk then you don't have the accurate outlook to be a credible writer. Worse is if you have seventeen completed novels but have never even bothered to submit any for publication. (And yes, I know that Emily Dickinson only published four poems in her lifetime and is still a literary cornerstone, but she wasn't a *professional*, and do you really want to live her life? ... unwilling to leave your house or stand in the same room with your visitors?)

J.D. Salinger can make a lifetime career out of one brilliant novel and a handful of shorter fiction. Thomas Harris can afford to take eight or nine years to put out a novel. The rest of us have to produce fairly quickly and write very efficiently.

Okay, so this isn't a game to you.

Writing, even if only for the small press field, means that you put your ego on the line every day of the week. You learn to live with the smirks of your friends and family—or their outright frowns and grimaces—when you tell them you're a "writer." You put up with them asking you how much money you've cleared when you've made a whopping $2.16 on your most recent sale or only gotten a handful of copies. When your Uncle Morris shrieks giddily, "What the hell are you going to do with that pitiful amount?" you want to tell him how you'd just love to clean out his throat with it.

And why do they smirk and sneer as much as they do?

Sadly, they've got a pretty good reason.

Writing is more than a profession, it's also an affectation adopted by those who do not write, or write very little, yet enjoy believing themselves to be artists. Here you are marketing your second unsold 100,000 word novel and some guy who's written two bad prose-poems for his creative writing class exercises is also telling people that he's a "writer."

You are a professional though because you act professionally and get the job done where it matters most—on the page. Your intentions are noble: you want to do the best job that you can, and you want to be read.

In college I knew a "writer" (it's okay to snicker in this case—in fact, I'd really enjoy it if you would) who claimed that fifty years after his death his progeny would open a trunk in the attic, discover his unsold manuscripts, sell them to a major publisher where they'd all become instant bestsellers, and he'd finally be acknowledged as an unheralded genius of the ages.

Pardonez-moi ma Francis, but I say that's pure grizzly shit.

Claiming you're actually an unappreciated sage of the century isn't only the last salve to one's brutalized ego, but it's also a conceit that only serves to undermine your own values and credibility.

So how do you put up with it?

How do you pull yourself together enough to put another story in an envelope and mail it off to yet one more magazine when you can feel your heart slipping through your ribcage?

How do you learn to live with rejection letters that are barely comprehensible and written by near-illiterate editors?

The answer is as simple to say as it is difficult to accomplish—you have faith in yourself.

You must realize that the struggles and setbacks are all part of the process. Getting rejected is a part of the plan, and so is being discouraged and angry.

It's difficult as hell to know what to do with your rejection letters when you first start getting them. Do you rip them up or wallpaper your bathroom with them? Are they worth the paper they're printed on? Should you actually listen to the comments?

Most editors don't have much time to comment on each individual story. If you're lucky you'll get a couple of kind sentences and some sort of reason why the editor is passing on your tale. Remember that it is not the editor's job to teach you to be a better writer. His only job is finding the best stories for his magazine. You shouldn't expect lengthy explanations on the strengths and weaknesses of your work.

However, if you do receive a drawn-out rejection, I suggest you listen to all the editor has to say with an open mind. Some editors can be incredibly helpful with their constructive criticism. Some can be vicious and degenerate, with their own axes to grind, who enjoy their position of power and like nothing better than to watch newer writers twisting in the violent winds of the small press. Over the course of your struggles you'll probably run into each type.

You are charged with remembering that all rejections are merely one person's opinion. Perhaps it's a professional opinion and perhaps it's not, but it's still only a single view of your work. If you can take something positive from the comments then do so, if you can't then leave them aside. My suggestion is that you save all rejection letters for the first couple years of your writing life, for one important reason. Eventually you'll be able to go through them and see how many of the magazines have folded up and blown away while you are still working towards your goals, meeting them, and exceeding them. It's a powerful validation, and one you deserve for continuing to strive forward.

You might expect me to put in here that it would be a wise move on your part to join a writer's group so you can share your sorrows with like-minded folks. Actually, I'm here to warn you away from most writers groups. For three reasons.

First: if the group is composed of only beginning writers they all might feel reluctant to actually give an honest opinion, especially if it's a negative one. Instead of furnishing a truthful critique they might feel inclined to simply give empty words of encouragement or a vacuous "This is great!" You need to know the difference between constructive, helpful advice and a vacant stab at support. That's going to take you time.

Secondly, some groups are made up of rabid complainers and naysayers about the publishing field. They tell you it's not what you write but who you know. They squeal that real genius will forever be buried beneath piles of worthless fiction and only sell-outs and hacks can get shelf space for their insipid rubbish.

You have enough travails of your own, and you don't need to deal with their despairing rancor as well. Take it from me, we've all got the same tales of woe. It's how we deal with those troubles that separate those who will continue forward and those who will stew in their own toxins. In any case, you're much better off not having to deal with these kinds of embittered folks at this early stage of your career.

Third: even honest critiques are difficult to deal with, especially when you're a beginner. You'll get a variety of opinions about your work, and you'll have no real idea about who to listen to or why. You'll sneer at wonderful advice and listen to soothing assurances that you're as good as any best-selling author out there, which may or may not be true. You'll face one member who loves the opening of your tale but hates the ending, and another who feels the exact opposite. Until you develop a certain security about your writing and understand your own narrative strengths and weaknesses, you might be best off staying away from opposing group dynamics like these.

Also: don't ask for comments if you're not ready to hear the worst. I don't necessarily mean nasty remarks about your story, I mean the worst kind of responses.

You might be smiling and bright-eyed and eager to hear what your sister Ellen has to say about your tale, expecting her to rave about your genius. Instead she winds up telling you, "I don't get it." Or, "Why don't you write something that people want to read! Write a happy story!"

Don't set yourself up for that long of a

fall. If your mother has never read a fantasy, horror or science fiction story, then don't expect to get anything more from her than a dazed look of confusion no matter how wonderful the piece might be. Others might give an accurate critique and find genuine flaws in your story—you have to be willing to keep an open mind and not drop into a well of frustration because you're not as perfect as you'd hoped.

So, exactly how do you combat discouragement? Write another story. How do you fend off depression over lagging sales? Write another story. How do you get by your own euphoria, giddiness, self-doubt or disappointment? Write another story, and try to make it even better than those that came before it.

Face the page.

Remember you're here not only because you want to be, but because you have to be.

Forget about everything else but the work that comprises your art.

WHERE DO YOU GET YOUR IDEAS?

or

Things to Say at a Convention if You Want to be Welded Into a Steel Drum and Kicked into the Okeefenokee

WELL, IT'S ABOUT THE DUMBEST QUES-tion in the universe besides "Whatever happened to Mayor McCheese?" but you should probably concentrate on what plot elements excite you mentally/emotion-ally and discover why. The fact remains that we don't know where our ideas come from—from inside, from outside, from our childhoods, our heartaches, our joys and fears. All of the above or none of the above. Nobody knows and I'm not even sure if anybody really wants to know.

Here are some possibilities though, and some workable ways to frame your own ideas:

Articles:

Horror writer Jack Ketchum kept a wide array of articles cut from daily papers from across the country to help generate ideas for his stories. A collated series of files on various topics and a lot of research documentation on a single subject can be extremely helpful. I think it's important though that you don't keep a box full of scribbled notes, shreds of magazine clippings, jotted words, phrases and random thoughts that won't make any sense to you upon a second viewing. I believe that a high number of *fragments* actually dilutes your ideas, thinning them into discarded bits and pieces rather than compiling them into a whole.

Don't overdo it. Find a subject that excites you and research it for flavor, but don't collect so much data that you've got five hundred pages of notes and no story or character. Consider how to apply what you find and learn.

Personal conflicts:

Conflict is the driving force behind all fiction. Do I use my own fears in writing my horror fiction? All the time. I also use it to create a viable context for my mystery plots as well, a driving force that propels my characters and the story action forward. My fears shift depending on whatever circumstances I'm currently in. It goes back to anxiety and dread more than anything that might be considered a phobia. Some folks crawl out of their skin at the idea of spiders or heights or enclosed spaces, and that kind of wellspring of emotion can be wonderfully useful in the narrative.

Most of my fears aren't as focused as that, although to me drowning and dying in a fire seem like pretty awful ways to shuffle off this mortal coil. I've used those images several times before. Usually my "fears" are just those things that cause me day to day stress, more than anything. Shame. Fear of failure. It allows me to give an emotional context to my horror fiction and an impetus to my mysteries.

Emotional turmoil is always the catalyst that gets the action of the work to move forward. I'm not much of a plotter *a la* Agatha Christie or Ed McBain. The stories I tell don't really need a variety of evidence and red herrings as scenario points. When I sold my novel *Shards*, my editor asked me if I could drop at least one more major clue into the mystery itself. I thought, "Well, just how in the hell am I supposed to go and do that?" It took me a long time pondering the story arc to work something into the natural unveiling of the mystery. I hate the "easy out" route that some crime novels choose, like the killer leaves a button behind and all the hero has to do is match the button to a coat and *voila*, the brilliant murderer who's escaped Interpol is caught. Too many authors rely on forced facts like that to wrap up their fiction, elements that don't occur naturally in the unfolding of the story and the characters.

Personal history and the fears and horrors of the past catching up to the protagonist are much more intriguing. It also allows me to dip into the well of my own life and mine various circumstances from my past to the fullest extent. Angers, failures, troubling incidents—I get to replay them and change the outcome if it suits my needs. A writer gets to live out all his fantasies within his work. Anybody I ever wanted to knock on his ass, I get to knock on his ass in my fiction. Those I never got a chance to apologize to or say "I love you" to, I finally get the opportunity to do so. Don't discount catharsis; you can have a lot of fun kicking the hell out of the punks from your freshman year in high school or falling into the arms of the unrequited love of your life.

Dreams:

This works for some people, but quite honestly, I don't remember my dreams or nightmares. Except for a few odd images here and there and an overall sense of anxiety at times, I can never recall anything I've dreamed. I wish I did, though, because it seems that some writers go to sleep and during the night all these great and extraordinary happenings occur. Their subconscious does a lot of the work creating stories for them, and they wake up with complex tales already sorted out and finished for them. So there's been no inspiration there, really, and conversely, I've never dreamed of matters I've written about. At least I don't think I have. Your best bet, of course, is to keep a notebook handy on your night stand so that if you awaken from a particularly vivid and intriguing dream you can get to work on putting down as much of it as you remember.

Daydreams are a different matter altogether, and where I believe the real work gets done. There are certain tales we run and rerun through our minds. Private fantasies, particular images, unfolding events that crowd together as story. Use your reverie and your musings, those thoughts that have been flowing around in your head for years. You'd be surprised at how much dramatic material you already have in your mind without ever thinking to put it down on the page.

If you one day hope to have three children and a dog named Rufus, a tow-haired husband and a kidney-shaped swimming pool, chances are you've imagined the details more fully than you've consciously realized. Don't shy away from those hopes and that introspection—use them to your best advantage. You've already got a starting point for any number of stories featuring Rufus and the kids and the pool. Run with it as you will. Nobody will be able to tell the difference anyway.

Reading:

There will be more on this later, but I'll give you the short course now. No, it's not plagiarism if you read a story or novel and find ideas there that fire your imagination and help generate more story lines. You need the influence of others to help you mine the depths of your own abilities and reach out towards plots, concepts, characterization, and greater possibilities.

Be careful though that you don't take a seminal story written thirty years ago and just change one minor arc of it, believing that you now have something fresh and unique to sell. If you're a science fiction writer, read dozens of novels in the field (as well as outside the genre) and try to discover what hasn't been written yet, what paths haven't been taken in the literature. I'm not saying that each writer needs to be groundbreaking in the extreme, but you can cross genres and mold techniques and style in an effort to come up with a form of tale that hasn't been told exactly the same way. Let other work influence you—don't be afraid that other writers' concepts are going to flow into your head. Use them and try to direct them elsewhere, making them your own.

TECHNIQUE, STYLE, AND WATCHING BOB'S FACE GET EATEN

1. Getting Started

IT'S ABSOLUTELY TRUE THAT YOU NEED to grab your reader's attention as soon as possible. Within the first few sentences and quite possibly within the first several words. That's not an exaggeration by any means. You've only got the opening two or three paragraphs of your tale to nab an editor's interest before he moves on to the next story or novel sitting in his slush pile. That's maybe thirty seconds of reading time. You might have the most brilliant story in the world from page two on, but nobody is going to know about it if they quit halfway down page one.

It's a natural process to learn about your

own character and story as you go along, developing the narrative and discovering the plot as you allow it to unfold. The story may stray from your original conception. It may wind and swerve and curve as you think of more plot twists.

The trouble with a great many beginning writers' stories is that they feel too comfortable taking their time getting into the piece. They introduce us to their protagonist, Bob, and describe in great detail his life at home: his soggy corn flake breakfast, his clothing, his wife, his job at the chemical plant, his four lovely children, including his six-month-old daughter Frieda. On page nineteen Bob finally gets Frieda to sleep, hops into his '95 Saturn to get a pack of cigarettes from the corner store, makes a wrong left turn, drives into a haunted town, and stares down the gullet of a vicious critter that eats the faces off good ole boys like Bob. Six thousand words used to describe what can be trimmed down to an actual three paragraphs of action.

One technique that I use to jump immediately into the movement of the story is making the first sentence as odd as possible. If it sounds extremely weird, then the reader will hopefully be intrigued enough to hold on for a few more paragraphs in the hopes of learning exactly what the hell the opening means.

Here's the first line of my science fiction-fantasy tale "I am a Graveyard Hated by the Moon": *Jombu, now the monkey-god Hanuman, son of wind, born to aid Rama in his battle against Ravana, golden-bodied with a ruby muzzle and a devastating roar, turned to me on the living ice and said, "Bum a cigarette off you?"*

I chose to open the story with a scene that is immediate, strange, full of concrete physical details, and yet contains several vital elements to how the tale will unfurl. It also gave me a number of factors that engaged *my own* imagination. When I wrote that sentence I had no clear idea where it would lead me, and that's the way I wanted it. The peculiarity allowed me any number of directions in which to move, and many possibilities as to its meaning.

Kurt Vonnegut mentions that you should "start as close to the end as possible." I think that's helpful advice that might easily be misinterpreted. It doesn't mean that you start with the hero holding a gun on the killer and the two of them discussing—through heavy exposition—all the things that have led them up to this particular moment. Some writers start so close to the end that their stories are only three pages long, and they keep wondering why they can't write lengthier pieces.

I take the stance that the story should start already in motion, with the characters presently caught up in some of the plot threads. You can fill in whatever details need to be supplied as the tale progresses. Don't spend those nineteen pages about Bob going through his lengthy normal daily routine before making that left turn and suddenly finding himself in a town of creatures that snack on his quivering nostrils.

Cleave off all the fat. Remove the non-essential. Keep only what's needed.

Leap into the fray swinging.

2. Narrative Voice

Some folks say that they can't read other novels while writing their own because the other author's voice tends to impede on them. If that's true then read *more*. If someone else's voice can supersede your own then perhaps you're not making the correct narrative choice in the first place. Your own voice has to be strong enough not to be dislodged by scanning a few pages done by another writer.

It's your presence that has to possess the page, the flow and flux of the language in your own rhythm.

Building a strong narrative voice also

takes time. Give yourself that time. Understand that writing is always an ongoing process, one learning experience after another. Hardly anyone goes to the page already knowing what needs to be said or precisely how to say it. It's a slow evolution of style and language. Over the course of writing numerous stories you discover your own strengths and weaknesses. You do your best to hone your abilities.

My first novel *Dark Father* had a lot of fire and imagination but not a whole hell of a lot of story structure or smooth writing style. In recent years I've become much more capable of fluidity and confidence in my narratives—which I think are two of the most basic tenets of bringing a story across successfully.

Also, remember that you are the master of the page—sounds odd, doesn't it? But you'd be surprised how many beginning writers forget that fact. They delay the entire process because they count on divine inspiration. Yeah right, sit around all day long watching the Rangers play at the Garden, just waiting for great ideas to come hurtling down from the depths of space.

If you expect plots just to arrive fully formed, or for characters to make themselves known by whispering streams of perfect dialogue in your ear, you'll be sitting around doing nothing but trading *Pokemon* cards for the rest of your life.

Your voice doesn't come to you, you must go after it.

You learn whether you enjoy projecting humor into your tale or keeping it terse and suspenseful. You find out whether you're good at highly languid and poetic descriptions or short choppy sentences that work without as much lyricism. Sometimes a first person point of view works and sometimes you'll prefer the omniscient point of view.

Don't be afraid to fail. If you're not satisfied with the shape and sound and structure of a particular story, yank out the threads and reweave them until you're more pleased with the end product. You'll discover that how you say something is just as important as what you have to say.

3. Atmosphere

No matter what genre you're working in, the milieu you create is an essential part of what makes a tale memorable. By my definition—which isn't everybody's—atmosphere is the overall emotional impression that is made upon the reader. I'm talking about the sensations experienced and imprinted in his mind as the story develops.

In creating a sense of horror, there's more to it than simply writing about what scares you; a writer needs a great deal of empathy and sensitivity in order to mine the fears of his own life, and also to understand the pain, terrors, and tragedies that others have suffered. Whether you're writing about giant spiders, insane killers, reincarnated warlocks, ghostly happenings, grotesque deviates or parasitic critters living in a child's spinal column, you need to connect to the reader on an emotional level first.

The milieu might be considered "disturbing," "unsettling," "terrifying," or "eerie": these are the end-product adjectives that a horror writer is hoping to make his reader feel. You do your best to affect others as well as yourself. The weirder you get the more you need to anchor the work in reality via other means: you need to give the reader a sense of normality no matter how abnormal the story gets. Learn to put everyday details into the piece, to fill the tale with elements of authenticity before breaking the mold. That allows for a carefully constructed structure of offbeat truth.

Anybody can write a story about malevolent spirits haunting the living, but can yours be as affecting as Peter Straub's *Ghost Story* or Richard Matheson's *Hell House*? There's been hundreds of vampire novels, but is yours going to enfold your reader as effectively as Poppy Brite's *Lost Souls* or Richard Laymon's *The Stake*? Maniacal serial killers are the proverbial dime a dozen in horror fiction, but will yours show the depth of homicidal psychosis as Jim Thompson's *The Killer Inside Me* or Robert Bloch's *Psycho*?

No matter how strong a plot line you have, or how realistically your characters are portrayed, the ambiance that draws the readers in, or fails to envelop them, is what they're going to remember the most. You need to tie the reader emotionally through concrete imagery, striking language, and a pace that grips them in total. You create milieu through precise detail, description, and sensuality.

No, you pervs, I'm not saying that your characters should all find themselves in Feudal Japan surrounded by tiny women in teakwood sandals. Neither do they have to slip into an East Village massage parlor to face well-oiled men and snarling women in six inch pumps wearing leather and chainmail.

Instead of using only your narrator's vision to depict the tableau of your tale, also use his remaining senses to develop the validity of your piece. It helps to build the landscape of your story in a more natural sensual fashion. It adds a great deal of texture to your narrative, allowing the reader to participate in the tale to a much greater extent. You want to draw your readers in entirely so that they forget they're merely reading a novel. Engage not only their minds but their bodies as well.

If you're writing a science fiction novel about an alien world, try to imagine what an assault that strange place would be on the senses. Your colonists wouldn't just notice three moons in the sky, they'd have to deal with poisons and perfumes in the air never before described. The food would be bizarre, the feel of otherworldly objects might cause different sensations in a person's flesh and mind. Okay, this is basic, I know, but it's still important.

Remember how well Frank Herbert illustrated the smell of spice, and the vicious sun and sand of Arrakis against Paul Atreides' body in *Dune*? How the sounds and scents of Spider Robinson's "Callahan's Place" stories populate the bar as much as the patrons? How the memorable guttural speech of Gully Foyle in the opening chapters of Alfred Bester's *The Stars My Destination* illustrates the character as much as the flaming crimson brand of a tattoo on his face?

Use all of the senses to build the distinct minutiae of your story. You've got five of them, and some of you mystics out there have a couple of extra ones too. Let them all filter into your work to help bring it to life.

4. Conflict

We've already talked some about using personal experiences and ardent turmoil to create the conflict that will propel your plot. Writing about what you know might not always be pertinent, but writing what you feel usually is. I've found that it's easier to use emotional reality to get to the heart of other content. Writing about what matters to you, what frightens you, what torments or delights you will propel the tale, and connect it to other elements. Getting under the skin is so much more difficult and intense that just clambering on top of it.

When you're writing fiction—especially genre fiction, I think—you can say all the right things in the right places, get back at your enemies, make love to every person you've ever dreamed of being with. Writing is a form of venting. You get to open the pressure valve. There were a couple of rough patches in my life where, if I hadn't been able to throw the (slightly distorted) details down on the page, I don't know what the hell I would have done with all those feelings rushing around inside my skull. One thing I've noticed about writers is that we might moan and rage and glare, but we don't very often wallow. We vent and go on to the following page: the next story, the next book, the next challenge.

You get to replay scenes from life and say all the proper statements you didn't think to make the first time around. That's an incredible lure of fiction, but at the same time the author must construct his characters as imperfect, sympathetic, and by turns foolish and flawed. It makes for a resonance. I can bring my personal capacity and faults to my characters and toy with them as I wish for the betterment of the story.

Okay, one last recommendation: you've probably already been hammered quite a bit about the *show, don't tell* rule. It's especially true when writing about these kinds of emotional upheavals we're discussing here. It's too easy to only say, "*Delores was really really mad that the monster had eaten Bob's face off.*"

Feeling is represented through physical

action, or the lack of it. No matter how much you want to describe love or sorrow or fear, you really can't do it. You can only show the cause and effects and dramatic discord of such emotion.

5. Signature

There are certain styles and voices I fall into more naturally, of course, but I try to mine new areas if I can. There are also particular themes and images that recur in my stories, either through personal interest or because I want to use them as a memorable signature of sorts, a stamp that marks the work as my own.

Religion fascinates me and disturbs me, and I often convey this in my fiction either through symbolism or simply through the subject matter. Recurrence of this sort is to be expected throughout an author's career. We gravitate to that which enthralls and inspires us.

It's also true I have what I call my "water stories." Since I grew up on Long Island and spent a lot of time at the beach, I suppose it's to be expected. We were talking about using personal fears before, and I mentioned that one of mine would be drowning . . . especially at night. It's such a forlorn and lonely thought. The vastness of the ocean is a powerful concept, beneath the waves in all that darkness. It sparks a great many ideas for me, a lot of primal urges and awe and panic which I can use in my writing. Other images I use repeatedly include dogs. Dogs are, to me, a connection for man to nature in a way, I suppose. They're domesticated animals but still very much a part of the wild, and can be downright spooky at times. You're sitting there watching television and your sleeping dog suddenly rolls over and starts howling at the ceiling . . . well hell, that's going to get your heart pumping. A dog can represent many things, too: friendship, attack, animal urges, complacency.

Almost everyone will find their own natural signature concepts and images. I think it's important, though not necessary, to have something that you can use as a seal or mark to make your fiction stand out. Edgar Allan Poe repeatedly returned to the notion of the premature burial. Crime writer Charles Williams' novels are filled with skippers and boats, based on his seaman's background. Poet Linda Addison uses "the Night Bird" as the core poetic icon for a number of her pieces. John Irving uses themes that revolve around abnormal families, children in danger, and the recurrent symbols of bears, private schools, and wrestling. Harry Crews uses the physically grotesque and freakish. These topics and emblems make the work immediately identifiable with the author.

Setting can also be used as signature. If western/horror/mystery writer Joe R. Lansdale wrote a story set in South Philadelphia, it simply wouldn't be a Lansdale story. He writes tales set in his home state of Texas, and uses the landscape to add a vibrancy and honesty that he wouldn't be able to get anywhere else. The setting becomes character, theme, and a memorable brand. Manly Wade Wellman not only set his Silver John the Balladeer stories in the Appalachians, but he even gave John the dialect of mountain folk. The fiction of John D. MacDonald and Carl Hiaasen has become nearly synonymous with Florida. Stephen King is not only Maine's bestselling author, but also its number one patron and chronicler. Raymond Chandler not only used Los Angeles as his setting, but his protagonist Philip Marlowe became a representation of early L.A.

6. Outlining

I outline to the barest extent, writing out and working with different threads to see which one might be the most appealing to me. More than anything though, I suppose my work is character-driven—the fears and weaknesses of the protagonist are generally what formulate the plot through which they move. As previously mentioned, I believe that's a hell of a lot more intriguing than simply having heroes investigate a murder that really has nothing to do with them. I find it more plausible and interesting if there's a connection, some seminal event in the characters' lives that draw them together.

In my mystery fiction I always have a subplot that has nothing to do with the major crime story going on. Something that might be considered minor but which has greater and greater ramifications as time goes on. In *Sorrow's Crown* there's a thread concerning a former high school football teammate of my protagonist Jonathan Kendrick. It seems that Jon dropped the ball during a big game and this former teammate is still stewing about it after ten years, enough to possibly start terrorizing Jon's girlfriend. Now, I personally know folks like this who still gnash their teeth over high school events, and I'm sure you do too. To a certain extent everyone carries their own past on their backs, and that's why it's so true and so understandable, and why readers can relate to that kind of thinking through the course of the novel.

While these sort of plots and sub-plots are initially easier to write about, they are harder to thread together as the novel progresses. My cursory outlining helps for me to find the direction in which I want to go.

One exercise I find helpful is writing out questions to myself: why would the killer act in that way? Where would the hero go after finding out his girlfriend is pregnant? Who does he talk to? Who could have planted the false evidence? Where are the police at this moment? Any story thread that I'm not absolutely certain about I tug on until it falls into place or I pull it out altogether.

I think the beginning writer is always best off working from a short-form skeletal outline. By "short form" I mean that you don't need to know every idea, character, and scenario even before you begin working. Keep it concise and condensed. Outline enough to get you started, and when you come to the end of that short form outline, sit down and think through the following sections of your novel until you have another basic plan you can proceed for the next few chapters.

If you feel the need to diverge from that plan, then follow your heart and your creative urges. Don't stick with something that you feel isn't keeping your interest. In the course of the writing you may generate a whole new kind of excitement by letting the plot flow in a direction you hadn't anticipated.

7. Self-editing

The sad fact is that a writer must also be a brutal proofreader of himself at all times. Yes, it's true, not only do you get reproached by editors, critics, and trenchant readers, but you have to be harder on yourself than any of them ever could be. You owe it to yourself and your work to make it as valid and smooth as possible. If a line sounds pretty but doesn't advance the story, then cut it. Writing is rewriting, revising and reworking. As poet Anne Sexton stated: "Writing is fucking hard."

How do you know when you're finally done with a piece? You really don't. You simply reach a point when you have to give it up. I think you should put aside the finished story for a week or two before submitting the piece to a market. Even that short amount of time will give you a much different perspective on your completed tale, and you'll be able to see logic flaws, plot holes, and other mistakes you wouldn't be able to spot otherwise.

Here's the short-list of some of the most common editing errors a beginning writer makes:

• *Word repetition.*

It's one of the easiest traps to fall into and about the number one oversight we're all likely to make, in my estimation. It's incredibly difficult to find the faults in your own work, especially where word repetition is concerned, but you have to train yourself to be aware that the problem may exist. When the writing is going well for you, and the paragraphs and pages are just whipping along, you tend to stick to certain words that come easily and most naturally to you. Rather than slowing down and fixing sentence structure up, you'll decide not to break your momentum and choose to go back later to fix the piece. In rereading, though, you probably won't notice that you used the adverb "suddenly" eight times across five pages, but a careful reader will.

•*Passive verbs.*

Watch out for all the times you use "was" and "were" while writing. "We were standing" instead of "We stood." And "I was running" instead of "I ran." It doesn't sound like much initially, but besides making the tone of your tale less active, you must also consider the word repetition. Six straight sentences of "I was" will eventually grate on your reader's nerves.

•*Switching tenses.*

It's easy to unintentionally switch from past tense to present tense. A number of writers might employ the "switch" to add style to their voice or to show a delineation of time or flashback. This works in sections or in alternating chapters, but not so well when bouncing back and forth from sentence to sentence, or worse yet, within the same sentence. If the monster "*chews on Bob's face and spits out the overgrown, thatch-like eyebrows*" then Bob's corpse shouldn't be described as "*dropped to the ground and exploded like an over-ripe tomato.*"

Do typos and manuscript mechanics really count? You better believe that they do. I've dealt with a number of beginner writers who felt that it didn't matter if they sent single-spaced, typo-ridden stories on without a word count. All of it counts to stand out either positively or negatively in an editor's eyes.

An editor immediately splits up his submissions into various "piles." Those that are written by well-known names will go to the top of the pile, and those that look professionally done will go next. All of the manuscripts written in crayon, typed on a ribbon that should've been changed during the Nixon administration, or photocopied thirty-two times so that the pages have a dull gray film concealing the words like mist on a Scottish moor will immediately be tossed back into the SASE with a rejection form.

Worse is if you find a petty editor who actually *enjoys* receiving improper and unsuitable submissions so that he can let off a little steam by red-penning your work. He wants to show you that you've misspelled the magazine's name, left off the word count, mis-numbered and stapled the pages out of order, used an 8-point script-style font, single-spaced the story, and left previous rejection letters attached to the last page. At the next convention you'll see him up on the editors' panel holding up your ms. as an example of what not to do.

Don't sabotage yourself.

Do everything you can to start off on an even ground with every other writer out there, and then let your work speak for itself.

SURE, I COULD BE A BESTSELLER BUT I JUST DON'T HAVE THE TIME

or

How Were You Able to Beat the Time-Space Continuum, Dr. Asimov?

Time Management

YOU HAVE THE SAME TWENTY-FOUR hours in the day as everybody else in the world. If you're looking for an easy trick to somehow squeeze an extra forty-five minutes in here or there, you won't find one. There is no secret. The only truth is that if you want to find the time to write badly enough—if you *need* to write—then you won't push that next story to the back burner. It'll stay in the front of your mind, forcing itself out, and when you get a free thirty minutes to work on the tale, you will.

Because you're your own boss in the writing field, there's no one to crack a whip or force you to punch a time card, nobody to slap you silly if you start playing the latest computer game or hit the Internet for three hours flitting from chatroom to chatroom under your secret screen name of *StudPuppy*. You have to want to put writing above everything else.

You make your own choices: you can pop a new Japanimation video in the player, grout your shower, put four coats of wax on your Mazda, go kayaking on your day off, and rearrange your shoes according to heel length. Or you can finish that story you've been working on and get it into the mail.

Some folks say that you can "steal" spare minutes by doing things like using a tape recorder to dictate ideas and dialogue while you're driving. I think that the only thing you should be doing while driving is driving. Can you imagine getting into a fender bender and the cop plays back your tape to hear: "*And as we descended the icy cliff I heard the shrieks of Fredrickson behind as the goat-God Aiela tore into his squishing bowels...*" You might wind up sitting on the side of the freeway a lot longer than you expected.

Here's one lesson that can help you keep moving forward: set smaller, realistic goals.

Joe Lansdale mentions that when he was starting out, after he got home from his day job, he wouldn't go to bed until he'd written at least three pages—that's maybe 750 words. Not ten pages, not eight, and not even five. Just writing two or three pages a day will add up much faster than you might think.

I'm not someone who can handle being at my desk for five hours straight. I prefer to write in blocks of maybe a half hour or forty-five minutes. I'm constantly taking a break from the writing before it wears me out. I watch television for a bit, read a chapter of a novel, then write. Call a friend, get online, and write some more. Hit the mall, wax the car, and write. In that way I manage to write all day long without burning out.

Another helpful hint is don't "carry over." If you miss your three pages then don't decide to do six the following day, and missing them, nine the day after that. Chances are you won't make your objective, and then you'll find your lofty goals beginning to buckle beneath their own weight.

Don't get discouraged if you can only do a single page, or even just a few paragraphs, every day. So long as you're progressing you are in the process of finishing your story or novel.

Focus: Stick to one project until you're finished. If you get bogged down with attempting to write three or four stories at once, you're likely to do much less work across the board than if you focused all your attention on a single piece.

If you commit yourself, concentrate, and continue to proceed forward, then nothing can stop you from making headway and getting the job done.

I'M A SCIENCE FICTION WRITER BUT I'VE NEVER HEARD OF HARLAN ELLISON, ROBERT SILVERBERG OR THIS DR. ASIMOV GUY

or

*Stop Watching Seinfeld Repeats and
Go Renew Your Library Card*

<u>Reading</u>

IF YOU WANT TO BE A WRITER YOU HAVE to be a reader.

Remember when I said that there weren't any rules to being a writer? ... and if there were they could all be broken? ... well, I'm breaking my own damn rule by telling you that this is one rule *you can't break*.

You've got to read.

Highlight that, folks. Double underline and asterisk it.

You must read.

Not only do you read to learn the art form, but also so you can experience the full range and impact of being a writer from the *reader's* perspective. Sometimes it's easy to become so caught up in the thrill of creation that you forget you're doing all of this *for somebody else.* You have to know how the words work when you're on the other side of the page. You read in order to master approach, arrangement and procedure, narrative and movement. It teaches you to experiment and discover.

Read outside of your chosen genre. Read whatever you can get your hands on. Not simply horror, science fiction, fantasy or mystery, but everything from classic literature to poetry to non-fiction. Some of the most tragic, surreal, potent, bizarre, and wonderful writing you'll ever read you'll find among the "mainstream" works of James Agee, Albert Camus, William S. Burroughs, Herman Hesse, Flannery O'Connor, Richard Brautigan, Kurt Vonnegut, Joseph Heller, John Steinbeck,

Thomas Pynchon, and Donald Barthelme.

I think John Irving is a phenomenal and poignant writer, and his novels have stirred me in ways no one else quite has. Noted horror writer and historian Jack Cady is also the author of *Singleton*, a mainstream novel that is overflowing with its humanity and deep-rooted American sensibility. I also consider Orwell's *1984* and Trumbo's *Johnny Got His Gun* to be two of the most powerful novels ever written, true classics in every sense of the word. I enjoy all genres and types of writing: classics to poetry to '50s science fiction, sword & sorcery, the pulps, Vietnam War stories and men's adventure novels.

It all counts in a writer's development, and the more one knows of other genres and material and story lines, the more themes he'll have on hand and the better he'll be able to grip and hold a reader's interest.

NETWORKING
or
'Scuse Me While I Kiss Some Ass

Conventions

WRITERS, TO A LARGE EXTENT, ARE A shy bunch, and initially the idea of going to conventions can be intimidating in the extreme. When you're first starting out and have only a handful of credits—or none at all—to come within a few feet of your own literary idols is both awe-inspiring and frightening. The first person I met at my maiden conference was the charming dark fantasist Ramsey Campbell, one of my favorite horror writers. He asked if I knew the way to the lounge, and I could do little more than point while staring bug-eyed and slack-jawed, praying that my tongue would one day curl back into my mouth.

Can you sell a novel or story without ever meeting a publisher/editor/agent face to face at a conference? Of course.

But as I like to point out to folks, if an editor has two well-written stories of nearly equal worth, and he personally knows one of the authors (and likes him), then the editor will be swayed to favor his acquaintance and choose him over a complete stranger.

It's not fair and it's not nice, but it is human nature, and for that reason you need to take this truth into account.

Conventions are also about the best way to break out of your own self-imposed solitude. You need to get away from the desk and take a intermission when you can, and conferences are a perfect way to escape your seclusion while continuing to work at building your career. You'll be widening your network of fellow writers and contacts in the field. Attending panels can give you the scoop on upcoming magazines, publishing lines, trends and shake-ups at various houses.

Conventions are an excellent venue to give readings, as well. So what if you stutter and freeze and mumble and sweat up there? Just about everybody is nervous when reading aloud, especially the first time. At least people will hear your work.

Besides being highly informative they're a hell of a lot of fun, too. This isn't all gloom and doom drudgery and labor. You not only get a chance to meet your favorite authors in your field but also a great many other people who are more or less at the same level in their writing career as you are. After you've acquired some sales you'll be heartened to discover folks who've actually read you before. You want to talk encouragement? . . . hey, you get no better boost in this field than listening to readers who genuinely enjoy your work.

The Web

The Internet is an amazing resource for connecting with publishing associates and publicizing your work.

Build up an email list of those who might be interested in learning when you sell a story. Don't badger folks, but if you send out, say, a bi- or tri- monthly newsletter stating recent publications and your upcoming stories, you'll generate a great deal of interest in your work. Put together a bookseller list so that when your first novel is printed you can let dealers know about it.

Visit e-zine sites and sign guestbooks. If you read online tales that you truly enjoy, take the time out to send a positive email and contact those writers. They'll appreciate it and you'll be introducing yourself to fellow authors.

Posting to message boards will allow you to converse with other like-minded folks all over the world and give you the feeling of being part of a larger community. Sit-in on online interviews and make yourself known to others in the field. Volunteer to give interviews and chats whenever you can. World-wide contacts can get you market information in other countries. These associations can lead to meetings at conferences and life-long associations.

Correspondence

Don't forget about the old-fashioned way of communication: writing letters. When I first joined the Mystery Writers of America and the Horror Writers Association, I scanned the membership directories and wrote half a ton of fan letters. All of those authors were extremely kind to me and their encouragement helped me more than any ten creative writing classes every could. Those letters are also my personal treasures, some written by legendary authors no longer with us: Robert Bloch, Karl

Edward Wagner, and Marion Zimmer Bradley among them.

Don't be afraid to be a fan: all authors need and appreciate them, and letting your admiration shine through will remind you as to why you got into this business in the first place. Through mutual appreciation of work, you can form long-lasting friendships with your own literary icons.

That, to me, is possibly the greatest enrichment of my life as a writer.

WRITER'S BLOCK &
OTHER HANG-UPS

or

*If the Page is Supposed to be Blank
Then Why's It Smirking at Me?*

THERE ARE MANY FORMS OF WRITER'S block, and most of them are normal to the process.

The "I'm Too Good for my Own Bad Ass" Complex.

You've just finished what you consider to be your masterpiece, sent it off to the highest paying market you could find, and now you have no idea how you can match the incomparability and divine perfection of that previous piece.

The "Why Try?" Complex

Horror author and Silver Salamander Press publisher John Pelan named this one for me after having discussed our favorite authors at length. You read a wonderful writer who affects you so deeply that upon completing their novels you fall into a funk and think "Why should I even try? I can never write as well as them."

Natural Resistance to Rejection or the "Please Don't Kick me in the Pancreas Anymore" Complex

Writing is lonely, often disparaging, ego-rupturing profession, and the more you write the more gun-shy you're likely become until you build up the hardshell.

Getting Over It

How to jump-start the process:

One way to break back into the page is to switch gears. Try writing in a different genre or a different medium. Writing poetry, even if it's bad, might prove helpful to you in getting back into your prose.

Do a non-fiction article for a magazine. Heading in a different direction will help you clear your mind enough to find your way home again.

Go do something else completely—go to the city and catch an off-Broadway play. Go para-sailing. Take your dog for a long walk around the lake. Visit your mother and try to ignore the fact that she's prodding you to go back to college and become a podiatrist. Aerobicise. Take a drive to the beach and lay out in the sun, with the smell of salt, seaweed, and Mr. Softee in the air. Go out with your buddies to a bar you haven't been in since you graduated college and get soused to the same old songs. Take the kids to Chuck E. Cheese and show them what being a Ms. Pac-Man champion really means. Hit a museum and stare at the Van Gogh Exhibit until your eyes water. Live your life that is outside of the writing, and when you get back to the desk you'll probably find yourself refreshed and invigorated to leap back into the page.

Try watching a couple of movies in your preferred genre. "What? Is he saying that wasting time watching movies is a good thing?" Hell yes, I am. Sometimes you forget that you're in this field not only to produce brilliant literature but also for personal satisfaction and enjoyment. If you're a horror writer, watch a few horror movies and recall how much you enjoy the domain. It'll help you into a positive, horror-writing mindset. Watching science fiction movies or a series from when you were a youth will remind you of your earliest passion and love for the genre.

Fun, kids, don't forget to have fun.

The word might have connotations of puppies and playgrounds and co-ed volleyball, but I'm talking about the elements that once made us wonder what was alive and dying out in the wind, when the roiling clouds broke over your hometown, and deep in the night you wondered who might be crawling behind your bedroom walls (anybody remember the flick *Bad*

Ronald?) and you couldn't get to sleep because you'd lay there thinking about what Father Damien Karras' face really looked like when he hit the bottom step and you'd see that clutching, bloody hand over and over again. Come on, I know you used to get a thrill out of listening to the opening strains to the theme song of *Battlestar: Galactica* and *Buck Rogers in the 25th Century.*

Get back in touch with your inner child (and don't you dare try to smack me for using that '90s pop culture psycho-babble term, I'm talking about something else here, something real). Your day to day love of the craft is most likely based on that sense of wonder you had as a kid, back when you dreamed of stories and didn't have to think about actually writing or selling them.

You've forgotten what a thrill it was to put together your Aurora models (even the crappy ones with the glow in the dark heads and hands) or read through a stack of *Werewolf by Night* or *Star Wars* comics, or watch *Space: Above and Beyond* and *The Twilight Zone* and *Dark Shadows* (I caught it again on the SyFy Channel yesterday morning, ye gods, what complete drek, I loved it), and run home so you could catch Giant Robot Week on the *4:30 Movie*, or rent six bad videos with a couple of friends for a dark October night of complete cheez-whiz delight for the express purpose that you *wanted* those flicks to suck, the crappier the better—hell, that was the joy of it.

You *deserved* it.

And you still do.

THE BRIEFEST OF
FINAL COMMENTS
or
*Shit, Where's All the Friggin' Secrets,
You Bastard?*

HEY, I TOLD YOU FROM THE ONSET THAT there weren't going to be any.

I write because I need to write. If I were on a deserted island I'd write in the sand with a stick.

And so would you.

Now, go get back to it, and no matter what happens, always be true to your art and yourself, and never let anyone steal your faith.

Welcome to hell.

Have fun.

ABOUT THE AUTHOR

Tom Piccirilli was the author of hundreds of short stories, novellas, three award winning books of poetry, and more than twenty-five novels, including *A Choir of Ill Children*, *Shadow Season*, *The Dead Letters*, and *The Last Kind Words*. He was a five-time winner of the Bram Stoker Award, two-time winner of the International Thriller Award, was nominated for the World Fantasy Award, and twice for the Mystery Writers of America's Edgar Award. Tom's novel *The Last Kind Words* appeared on USA Today's bestseller list.

OTHER TITLES IN THE
NOVELETTE SERIES
from Fairwood Press:

The Jonah Watch
by Jack Cady
trade paper $17.99
ISBN: 978-1-933846-79-8

The Experience Arcade
by James Van Pelt
trade paper: $17.99
ISBN: 978-1-933846-69-9

The Sacerdotal Owl
by Michael Bishop
trade paper: $17.99
ISBN: 978-1-933846-72-9

*Seven Wonders of a
Once and Future World*
by Caroline M. Yoachim
trade paper: $17.99
ISBN: 978-1-933846-55-2

Amaryllis
by Carrie Vaughn
trade paper: $17.99
ISBN: 978-1-933846-62-0

On the Eyeball Floor
by Tina Connolly
trade paper: $17.99
ISBN: 978-1-933846-56-9

**80+ More Titles Available at:
www.fairwoodpress.com**

www.ingramcontent.com/pod-product-compliance
Lightning Source LLC
Chambersburg PA
CBHW020955030426
42339CB00005B/111